CW01084409

Relentless

by

Lee Headington

DORRANCE PUBLISHING CO., INC.
PITTSBURGH, PENNSYLVANIA 15222

ISBN: 978-1-4349-0266-5

Printed in the United States of America

First Printing

For information or to order additional books, please write:
Dorrance Publishing Co., Inc.
701 Smithfield St.
Pittsburgh, Pennsylvania 15222
U.S.A.
1-800-788-7654
www.dorrancebookstore.com

Dedication

I would like to dedicate this book to my brother, Chris, who was with me the whole time I spent writing this book.

I love you, Bruv.
R.I.P.

Newborn

Your first experiences as a child should be the ones of your parents acting silly in front of you. Making funny faces at you and blowing raspberries, putting their thumbs on their temples and waving their fingers in a funny manner. When you have older brothers, you'd expect them to play fight with you and protect you from anything that they thought would harm their little brother. What I witnessed was completely different and on top of that, the worst was yet to come. They say it happens in threes. What was that, then—good luck or bad luck? Well it sure as hell wasn't good luck. This book is going to be about my life. Through my childhood. Up to my teenage years and finally into adulthood.

As a child, I had to grow up really fast. I wouldn't have thought for one minute that I would ever experience my own parents' divorce, or the violence within my own family. When things get too much for children to cope with, they have an imaginary friend they can talk to. Someone like Rick Mayall from Drop Dead Fred or a teddy bear or a dragon. I felt like I had no one. All I felt was that I had me and only me. If bullying at school wasn't enough, I had to get it at home to. My one and only sanctuary. From the earliest age, all I can remember was violence. I can't remember how young I was but all I remember was seeing my brother Robert hiding behind the living room sofa and he was crying. The look of fear on his face and the look in his eyes was something that I'd never seen and not something I was ever going to forget. That experience is going to remain an unanswered mystery. I would have liked to have known why my brother was cowering behind that sofa. There were things happening that I couldn't understand back then. As I look back now, maybe the past is best left alone.

There are different types of screaming. Screaming when you watch a horror film or screaming when you ride a scary fairground ride or roller coaster. Nothing was more frightening when I heard the screaming coming from inside of my own household and it wasn't the last time I was going to hear it either. I was so scared that I put my duvet over my head in the hope that whatever it was wouldn't come into my room and get me too. Every time I heard that screaming, I would grab hold of my quilt, put it over my ears, and try to block out the sound of it. I was terrified. I wouldn't come out of my room until my mum came and got me. Then and only then did I know it was safe to come out of my room.

Everything in our house wasn't quite right.

A History of Violence
Pistols, "Friggin' in the Riggin'."

When my brother Robert was alive, he used to have a huge gang of friends. Most of them were real Cro-Magnon looking bastards. They were from the eighties era. They grew up listening to the Sex Pistols, Adam Ant, and Toyah. I have listened to one of the songs from the Sex Pistols "Friggin' in the Riggin'." I found it to be quite an aggressive, nasty song. I'm sure that is what fueled my brother's aggression. He also used to watch lots of horror films which consisted of vampires, werewolves, and many other demons from hell. One of his favorite haunts was Cadbury Woods. That indeed was a very dark place. He once had a party up there with some of his friends and his best mate decided to follow them up there. Both my brother and his best mate, Wayne, thought it would be funny to jump out on the women up there so they gathered a long dark coat, a balaclava, some paint, and a machete. When everyone was deep in conversation, Wayne smeared the paint over the balaclava and ran through the fire which my brother lit for full effect, brandishing the machete over his head and screaming like a maniac. That's enough to make anyone have a heart attack. One of the girls started to cry, she was that affected by it—and who can blame her? I wouldn't want to have been there at the time.

These are the things that made my brother really happy but I think in a way it played a big part in my brother's behaviour. Fierce and angry most of the time he was. He was outside in the garden one morning, digging it over with a garden fork. He was having a chat with one of his mates when he drove the fork deep into his foot. I didn't even hear him scream in pain. He came in afterward, hopping through the house.

I was eating my breakfast at the time when he pulled off a piece of flesh and flicked it at me, which he found highly amusing. I don't care what anyone says about my brother. He will always be known as a hard bastard to all his friends and the people he has met. And nothing will ever change that, never.

One night when my mum was drinking I asked her about the night my brother and my dad had a huge fight in the living room. She finally told me her version of events. He had his hair cut by one of his friends. As he was a punk rocker, he wanted a Mohawk as I was told but I remember seeing it myself when I was younger so I know that was true. He also had it dyed bright orange. He was really pleased that he had his hair done, even more that my dad was about to see it. I'm not sure if he wanted a reaction from my dad or whether he was pleased to show it off—this is another one of those questions that remains and always will be unanswered. My mum told me that my dad had a few friends over for some drinks and a social gathering. I was told that my brother walked in and showed our dad his new hairdo. In response to my brother's fashion statement Dad replied, "What the fuck have you done to your hair?" My dad must have felt a little embarrassed by it. He walked himself and my brother out to the living room and my mum said that my dad began to punch my brother round the face and head. My dad walked back into the living room wanting to forget about the whole experience and continued the conversation with his friends. My brother on the other hand didn't say a word and calmly walked upstairs and into his room where he kept knives, knuckles spikes, nunckers, and swords. One of which he used to attack my dad with. My brother walked down the stairs and into the lounge where my dad was sitting. He started with an overhead lunge and my dad picked up the small coffee table to stop himself getting seriously injured. I think the result would have been unthinkable. The sword made short work of the coffee table. My dad ran into the dining room and there was an even bigger table in there and my brother started hacking away at that. (I know this to be true because when I came down the next morning the table was missing some edges.) My dad ran upstairs and put the heavy sewing machine at the bottom of the door so my brother couldn't get in. If this was true then I couldn't imagine the thoughts going through my father's head, almost having lost his life to his own son, whom he had helped bring up. My other brother, Chris, kept a cricket bat by the side of his bed that night just in case Robert wanted a go at him. A cricket bat against a sword has got more chance than a small wooden coffee table. The next morning, when I came downstairs I saw some spots of blood on the walls in the front room and the dining area. I asked my mum if anything happened last night and she replied, "Yes, Robert attacked your dad with a sword." A little later I walked upstairs and found my dad. I also saw the sword imbedded in a side cabinet. My dad was trying to pull it out so he could get rid of it, which wasn't a bad idea since he almost lost his life against this piece of metal.

My mother's version of events is totally different than my father's. My mother's was more graphic than my dad's. My dad said he was walking through the playing fields and saw my brother. Robert apparently said, "Come on then," and it went on from there. I will only say that I remember seeing the sword, the cabinet, the blood on the walls, and my brother's haircut so I can't be sure.

When I was getting bullied at school, my mother used to write letters to tell the school officials about my getting bullied. My dad now says that he wished that I would have gone to him and told him what was going on. The thing was, I was too frightened to tell him just in case he thought it was my fault again. I just didn't want another beating, so I never told him anything and I just bottled it up as my mum's letters weren't doing anything. I never even told him about the dark figure that used to torment me late at night, just in case that was my fault too. So I just lived with it.

When I found out that my grandfather was violent towards my own father and grandmother, it was obvious that it was a vicious circle. When you grow up in that environment then that is all you know in life. I now understand that my dad didn't really have much of a father-son relationship and may have found my behaviour hard to deal with. Maybe that is why I copped a beating.

Brotherly Love

I used to be quite envious of my sister. I felt that my brother Robert loved my sister more than he did me. Maybe it was the fact that he already had two brothers and never knew how it felt to have a sister. Another question unanswered. I remember when he had taped an episode of the Thundercats, which I absolutely adored. I would watch the cartoon every day on BBC1 after I came home from school. When I found out Robert had recorded this cartoon, I was so pleased that he might let me watch it. One night when he was about to play it, I was told to go up to bed. So I went up to my room but I thought they were playing with me so as I heard the theme tune come on I crept downstairs and I walked into the front room and they all hurried to switch it off and I got a telling-off for it. I thought to myself, What have I done wrong and why were they being so cruel to me? I also remember the cartoon called *He-Man and the Masters of the Universe*. I collected all the He-Man action figures as I did those for the Thundercats. There was one figure from He-Man I was missing and my brother had it in his possession. He knew how much I wanted it but he never gave it to me. He used to wave it in front of me, taunt and tease me with it. It was so hurtful and on top of that he played me off against another person who used to hang around with me. I can't remember why but one day I, my brother, and this other person were all in the same room and instead of giving me the figure, he gave it to the other person and together they both laughed at me. Why I don't know, but when I went round to see the other person, I stole it off of him and I made sure that he knew it.

I remember coming down the stairs one morning and when my foot touched the last stair, my brother jumped out on me. He used to terrify the life out of me when he did that. So one afternoon I noticed that he had his back to me and I thought it would be great to get even. He was standing on the old football-club step, talking to his friends. So I crept up behind him and as I was just about to make him jump, he kicked me in the face like a horse would do. He launched me about ten feet in the air and I came back down and slammed on the ground. Good thing it was grass. But it was still hard. Anyway, as I got up I cried my eyes out from the shock of it all and my suffering from the pain. I ran home to tell my mum what had happened but my brother just ran after me. He picked me up and took me back down the playing fields to calm down I suppose. I don't know what I did to deserve that. I also didn't know what I did to deserve him throwing a handful of tea leaves in my eyes. He must have really hated me for some reason. Maybe he was pissed off at me for something.

I was so angry with him for all the bullying. So I dug up our beloved cat Mitsy, more his than mine. I started kicking her around the garden as I didn't have a football. I knew what I was doing was wrong but I didn't care. The anger I felt was so blinding that I didn't think about anything else. I don't know how he came to find out but he asked me who was responsible for it, so I blamed it on one of the other kids from around our estate who bullied my sister once, and revenge was sweet. Anyway I didn't feel like copping a beating from my brother— but I think the other kid did get one!

The Boogie Man

Everyone has a personal boogie man, which can take shape in many different forms. I didn't know what type of boogie man mine was—I thought it was Dracula at first, but to be quite honest, I didn't know and I didn't care. I just wanted it to leave me alone. At that time I used to share a bedroom—the smallest in the house—with my sister, Lesley. Our beds were on the opposite side of the room; mine was on the left and my sister's was on the right. I woke up in the middle of the night once. I looked over to see if my sister was still awake but she was fast asleep. As I was about to roll over, I noticed something dark by the bedroom door. I couldn't make it out as I had just awakened and my sight was a bit blurry. But as I looked again, it was more like a figure was standing there looking at me. I thought I was dreaming at first but I wasn't and I was so scared that I put my covers over my head in the hope that it would go away. About two seconds later I felt someone or something poke me. I was terrified. I went into a cold sweat and I started to panic. When you go into a state of panic, it's almost as if someone has their hands around your throat and is choking you. I couldn't cry out for my mum or dad as they were fast asleep and wouldn't have heard me anyway.

After the first night I was hoping that it would never come back but I was very much mistaken. It came back many times after the first night. I couldn't describe how I was feeling. It's not something as a child you imagine happening to you. My brother used to rent horror films and I felt like I was being forced to watch them with him. They are all about monsters eating people. I didn't say anything to my parents as I thought that if I did then the creature would come and get me and it would be worse than before, so again I bottled it up and I didn't tell a soul. Although this was happening to me, I found myself being drawn to it. I wondered where it came from and if it was real. When I reached my teenage years, I would wake up and look over at the door to see if it was there. It never returned as I got older. Sometimes I would even miss it and I hoped that it would come back but it never did. I think it was better that it didn't.

Robert

Before I was born, my dad, my mum, my brother Chris and my brother Robert shared a house in Kingston Seymour. It's a small community. You really wouldn't call it a village or town because there are no shops there. I used to go fishing with my dad there quite a lot which is what I enjoyed doing; the only thing I didn't like was that it was really cold, every time I went.

Sometime in 1974 or 1975, my family moved from Kingston Seymour to Yatton. This was when my sister and I came into the world. I think the building we then occupied was built in the late 1930s to early 1940s. There was only one other family who occupied this dwelling before us. It was a three-bedroom, semi-detached house. Each of us had our room to sleep in but Robert preferred the loft, as it was dark up there with lots of spiders. He made lots of friends in Yatton and other far off places too. It's actually impossible to know just how many friends he had. But it was a lot. My dad had a full-time job, as did Chris, and Robert had a part-time job at the chicken farm in Claverham. He once took me along with him to show me what it was like. The only thing I remember about that day was the baby chickens. My brother was really gentle in the way that he handled them. I enjoyed that day with him.

On another occasion in our back yard, but again, it was one of those days I don't remember too much of. I do remember the packet of salt and vinegar crisps I had in my hand and that Robert took about three photographs of me. I will always remember that day. It was one of a few happy moments I shared with Robert. Even though he was quite a ruthless kinda guy, he cared and those are the words you would never hear him say. He gave us some of the best Christmases that we ever had. He used to do a lot of pinching from the local woods to get the Christmas trees and the local allotment just so we could have food on our table. He used to go to Cadbury Woods, hunting for what he called food. My sister and I even had a taste of Robert's creatures. I remember the squirrel he hung on the washing line. It was all tense and you could see the muscles on its body as it hung there. He once brought a fox home as well. I remember when he and some of his friends tried to cut its stomach open with rusty knives. They tried so hard to cut it open. They finally got it open but my brother only wanted the liver; I don't think he ate the whole carcass—well I don't remember him eating it. I thought that was the last thing he was going to bring home but I remember seeing a dead sheep in our back garden too. He never ate that, though. I also remember when he decided to take up driving. His first car was a Morris Marina. Blue and a very old thing it was. He took his best mate out in it and even he said he would never get in while my brother was driving. That night he plowed into a neighbour's car. Everyone thought it was funny. My brother didn't, but he didn't care— he just ran off and left it.

Robert had a very fearsome reputation and there weren't too many people who wanted to get on the wrong side of him. He would tease me with black plastic spiders and dangle me over the stairs by my ankles and swing me to and fro. I would scream my head off for him to stop doing it. It used to terrify the life out of me. He also used to jump out on me at the bottom of the stairs.

Robert had a dark sense of humour. He wasn't alone with that as he had his best mate living across the road. Living opposite each other, they would both flash their torches to signal one another. Together they made quite a pair. They would hang around at the youth club. Some of the things they did were crazy. His best mate did a flying head butt on this other guy whose motorcycle helmet was brand new. Anyway this guy dared him to do it, so he ran from one end of the club to the other, headbutted him and knocked him out. Laid out cold.

They did everything together and I mean everything. They would get drunk, steal, womanize, beat up anyone who got on the wrong side of them. They would also go to the nearest town for a good punch up. Even other gangs came up from Weston or from other areas in the southwest for a ruck. But my brother and his best mate—oh, and not forgetting his gang—would send them all packing. They were Yatton's nightmare. Nobody will ever live up to what they did. There were a lot of guys who would call my brother their best mate. He had quite a following. Lots of women fancied him. There was only one woman for him though: Gill was her name but I can't remember her surname.

Robert was also really friendly with the police. They were frequent visitors to our address. There was one police officer with whom my brother got on really well. P. C. Barrett. I remember when I was down the playing fields and saw them both walk the whole perimeter as they talked. I don't know what that was about and I'll never know. P. C. Barrett was quite an understanding guy and I think he must have took a blind eye to some of the things my brother got up to.

One night Robert and my father had a huge bust up. Robert sought sanctuary in Cadbury Woods. He must have stayed there for about a month. I and my sister used to go up there to visit him. He slept next to this massive oak tree. When I was there I looked up at this huge tree; I had this really warm feeling that this tree was looking after my brother. To know he was staying there every night and the fact that he had this tree for company made me feel a little better and that he wasn't alone. Next to where he was staying was a huge tip for everyone's rubbish. As much as I hated that place, it had some really cool stuff, like BMX parts. which was the only reason why I went up there. I remember one night when Robert and some of his mates went up there to see if they could get a wheel for my brother's bike, since his was broken and he needed it to be fixed so he could ride to work. After much searching he finally found what he went up there for so we headed back. As we were walking away, I noticed some "cats"—they were actually rats. They were huge, even bigger than a cat. Good thing we were walking away from there. On the way back, however, it started to get dark. We were walking towards the cricket ground when we all heard this dog barking but we couldn't see where the dog was. The barking got louder and louder as the dog came running towards us. One of my brother's mates chucked me up on the cricket ground and all of them joined me apart from Robert. As we started looking for him he came out of the darkness and was hiding in the trees with this wheel. He said, "If that dog came near me I would have smacked it around the head with this wheel." Everyone laughed as we all walked home. That was a good night and I enjoyed spending it with my brother.

Something wasn't right with my brother, I could sense it. When he returned home, my dad moved out. They spent some time chatting in the living room. I know this because I sat on the bottom stair trying to listen to what they were saying but was unable to hear them clearly.

When I came down on one particular morning, I walked into the front lounge where Robert was. He was just looking into space. I said "morning" to him—to which he replied, "morning. Lee," as he lifted his head and smiled at me. He would go to his room when it was time for bed. We all didn't know it but he was suffering in silence. He was in so much pain but he didn't mention it to any of us. As he was a hard bastard, the only thing I could put it down to was that he thought it might have been a stomachache or something and it would eventually pass; but it never did, it just got worse and worse. In the end he went down to the doctor's to see what it was. I don't know how he came to find out but he had contracted cancer. Nobody knew just how bad it was. Or how he got it. But I think it had something to do with that tip.

I don't how old I was when I was told about it. At the time I didn't know what it was or indeed that it was responsible for so many deaths in this country. My brother had the worse kind. It started from his groin area and eventually it spread through his body like wildfire. Nothing could stop it. Maybe if he went to the doctor's a lot earlier they could have done something for him but I don't think they had the technology back then. My brother was admitted to hospital in Bristol about a week or two later. I went with my mother to visit him once. We sat waiting for him in the visitors' room for five minutes. When he came in and sat down we started chatting—well, my mum did all the talking, I just sat there and looked at him. Even though he had contracted this terrible disease, it didn't stop him from having a sense of humour. When he made the nurses up there cups of tea, he added a colouring additive to their cups, so when they would finally get their cup of tea it was usually green, red, blue, or yellow. They didn't seem to mind—they loved my brother up there.

All of this was taking its toll on my mother. All she did was drown her sorrows in a glass of sherry or a two-liter bottle of cider. She would even turn up at the hospital after she had been drinking and this used to embarrass my brother, so when my dad went to see him he told my dad not to bring her again if she had been drinking. He came home for half the day. I, my dad, my sister, and my brother Robert all went out for Sunday lunch. We all had a big silver tin with roast potatoes—a funny lunch I know but I didn't care; I was with my brother. When the day finally came to a close, my dad was ready to take my brother back to the hospital. As they were about to leave, my brother raised his thumb, as did I. Little did I know that it was going to be the last time I would ever see him. Sometime afterwards, I was asleep in my bed when my sister came in and told me to get up because my father wanted to talk to me. Deep down I knew what it was about. I didn't feel like getting up but I did. I got dressed, walked down the stairs and into the front lounge where my mother, my dad, my sister, and my brother Chris and his new girlfriend, Sharon, were. My dad told me to sit down next to him. As I sat down he said, "I got some terrible news. Robert passed away." I just burst into tears. I didn't want to believe it. As I sat there crying, the sun was shining and it came straight into my face. I think somehow that it was my brother Robert and he was telling me that he was happy where he was and that he finally found peace.

Robert Thomas Headington
1965–1988
R.I.P.

My Mum

I shall never know the real story behind my mum's upbringing. I know that her grandmother took care of her. Why I don't know. I've never met my mother's parents. I have been told that her mum and dad left her in dirty nappies and fed her sour milk, but, I was told by somebody else so I'll never know if it was true. My mum never really talked about her parents all that much. She did however talk about her half sister. All I got to know about her was that she was a bit of a bully towards my mum. She used to tell me that every day she was in school she would always have to defend herself—that was, until she picked her up by her throat and told her to leave her alone. She told me she never got any more hassles from her half sister again. How your own sister can bully you all day every day is completely unbelievable.

There was one happy memory my mom told me about. It was about some really nice shoes that didn't fit her but which she bought anyway. She walked all day in these shoes. I can't remember how or why but her grandfather picked her up with her shoes on because they hurt so badly but she didn't care. It was a happy memory that I can say I'm pleased that I got to share with her. When I used to stay home from school, I would accompany her down to the local supermarket. I can remember walking back home with her and carrying the shopping. When it was finally put away, I and my mother would sit down. She would read a book and I would be eating a beef and tomato whilst watching Bugs Bunny and Daffy Duck cartoons. Those were the days I really enjoyed with my mum and to be honest, when I look back, I really felt that she was my mum.

She used to walk me into school every morning with one of the other neighbours, who also had a son. Together we would all run to the local bakery and pull each other's hoods to get in front of one another. Sometimes the son would beat me and some mornings I would beat him.

I also remember one day when I was about to go round another lad's house when I was in junior school. For some reason, I started to cry and I ran to my mum; I grabbed hold of her and I never wanted her to let me go. No offence to the other lad but I just wanted my mum that day. He was someone I felt was really one of my true friends in that school. He never bullied me or anything. He did however give one of the bullies a bit of a beating, so deep down I was pleased. The only thing I feel guilty about was that I never took the chance to go round his house for tea. My sister went to the same school but she left because she was bullied a lot like me—but it was by this one particular cross-eyed, ginger freak of nature. (I hope you rot in hell.)

My sister then started a new school, but it was an even more violent school than the one I was in already. On the last day of my school, all the kids in the same year had the chance to go and sit in the next class that they were going to move to. I sat in the other class waiting for the day to end, which was going to be my last day in that hell hole they called a school. All the kids bullied me and none of the teachers helped me—can I just take this chance to say thank you very much? It was my mum who gave me the chance to go to that new school. I was really pleased that I went there. It may not have been an ideal school but everyone left me alone most of the time. I got to make some great friends and I wouldn't change that for the world. My mum used to let some of my friends from that school stay over for the weekend. There was this one kid who I let stay round; he was from one of the other neighbouring villages. We had become really good friends. We would go in the woods hunting together for pheasants and rabbits. We never did catch anything though. When my dad left and my brother died, this other kid's father took an interest in my mother. I remember when they all came round to visit us. My friend, whom I hadn't seen for a long time, his brother, and their father—with some of their friends—would knock on the door after they all had been drinking at a pub which wasn't far from our house. My mum and sister would be a little miffed about them coming round. My mum never really liked this sort of attention from this other kid's father. She never really told me why, and to be honest I got fed up with it. Maybe it had something to do with him being an alcoholic.

Not too many people came round to our house after the death of my brother. My sister was involved with this guy who was an absolute loser. My mum used to think he was okay and as my sister was happy with him it didn't really bother her. He wasn't liked around the village that much and everyone had a go at him every chance they got. He used to hang around with his own circle of friends who used to stay round our house. They all seem to be obsessed with my sister for some reason. I just wished they all got a life and left ours alone. A couple of them were nice and they have been really good friends ever since.

Sometimes I wish there was something more I could have done for my mum. As I was in school, there wasn't a lot I could do. My mum just seemed to be really pissed off sometimes. I never really knew the reason behind it. When I look back, I wonder what those prescription tablets of hers were for. I know she wasn't eating much. I didn't even notice and when you are at such a tender age it's not something you should have to worry about. She seemed to care less and less about what I got up to. One night I stayed out and didn't return until the next morning. I was with another person but I could easily have been taken. I think she just gave up caring. I started to steal things from our local supermarket; the gardening centre was where I got most of my trees from, but someone followed me and told me to dig up what I had planted. I was also in the company of my sister's ex-boyfriend who showed me how to steal and how easy it was. When I look back at what I did, the reasoning for it was because my mum was getting worse and I didn't know how to deal with it or indeed how to cope. Every morning I used to pop my head round my mum's bedroom door and ask her if she would like a cup of tea; she replied with a "Yes please, Lee." After I made it for her, I would sit cross-legged on the floor next to my mum to hear how much she loved her cup of tea. Every sip she took she said, "That's nice," over and over again. So when I started to hear this, I thought to myself that this was making my mum feel better, so every time she asked for a cup of tea I would make it without fail.

After my brother's funeral, there must have been more than fifty people there who had come to pay their respects and to say their last goodbyes. When we all got home, there was a knock at the door and I was the one who answered. In all the 365 days of the year they had to come round on the worst day possible. They were some preachers from our local church. They said, "Is your mother or father home?" I went and got my mum. I followed her to the front door where the people from the church tried to start a conversation with my mum about Jesus and how he is the Saviour of humanity. After listening to this for about two seconds, my mum interrupted them and said, "I don't believe in God because he just took away my son!" They looked at each other and before they could say anything else the door was slammed in their faces. My mum went walking through into the living room with an angry face and said a few words in disgust. I also remember this really annoying guy in our house who kept saying, "Me and Wayne, Wayne and Me," like they were all of a sudden best friends. Wayne looked over to me and winked as if to say, "Yeah, in your dreams, pal." I noticed that this was all taking its toll on my mum and at the time she was emotionally fragile. One afternoon when I was about to walk downstairs, my mum was walking up towards me and I said, "You okay, mum." She just walked past me and it was if she didn't even notice me standing there. She didn't say a word and walked into her bedroom with a bag of my brother's clothes which she had from the hospital. She emptied the contents of the bag all over her bed. She grabbed a handful of my brother's clothes and put her face into them. As she did so, she fell on the bed and cried her heart out and as I stood there and watched from the landing, I knew at that moment that I was going to lose her forever.

When Christmas came round, it was a hard time. My mum used to miss my brother Robert a lot over the festive period. I used to write this huge list of toys that I wanted but I knew I was never going to get them. I remember when my brother Chris bought me a tool box for Christmas. I would have said it was the best present I'd ever had when I was at that age. Everything else from then on was a blur. In the middle of that year was when the shit was really going to hit the fan. I can't say I ever noticed a change in my mum or her drinking. I knew she liked to drink but I didn't think it was that severe. When she was starting to be sick, I used to get really scared and I phoned Dr Nelki, who came round on two occasions. I was later told that if she kept this kind of drinking up she wouldn't survive; but as she lost one of her sons I didn't think she cared much. I remember when she said she should have gone before any of her children. My dad came round on a few occasions to tell her to try and stop drinking so much but all this fell on deaf ears. The worst night of my life was on its way.

Early one morning I was awakened by the sound of my mum being sick in the bathroom again, but this time it was different. After she had stopped being sick I heard her say, "It's just a little bit of blood; I'll be all right in the morning." Then I could hear her walk into her room where my bed was. The next thing I heard was a thud, so I turned on the light and she had fallen to her knees and she'd hit her head on the chest of drawers. She looked at me with blood coming from her mouth and a scared look in her eyes which I'll never forget. I ran into my sister's room to wake her up. My sister said that she dreamt that this was happening. When I woke her up I said that there was something wrong with mum so we both ran back into my mum's room. My sister said to go and get one of the neighbours who was best at things like this, so while my sister was helping my mum to her bed, I ran downstairs and for some reason I couldn't open the door—I just froze. My sister then looked at me and ran out and got the neighbour instead of me. Five minutes later, they both returned and ran upstairs to see my mum. The neighbour rang for an out-of-hours doctor when clearly she needed an ambulance—which I was annoyed about to say the least. I know what I was about to do was wrong but I just wanted to see just how bad the situation was so I looked in and I could see that she had been coughing up blood in the sink and toilet. I could also see her handprint on the side of the bath where she had tried to support herself. That was something I was never faced with and I hoped I would never face again. I also wanted to share it with my mum so she wouldn't feel like she had gone through it alone. The ambulance was finally at the house and they took one look at my mum and took her away. My dad was called early in the morning to be informed of what had happened. As I walked downstairs, I saw my sister crying in the living room and the neighbour was consoling her. I just walked into the front lounge and stood in front of the television and fell to my knees. Then I heard this little voice in my head saying, "Lee, you're going to be alone for the rest of your life." Then my dad walked in. He said, "You all okay Lee?" So I said, "Yeah." That voice confirmed it.

About a week later, I and my dad went up to the hospital to visit my mum. When we got there she was hooked up to a life-support machine with tubes coming out of her from everywhere. I just sat there and watched her. She looked so peaceful as she was sleeping. My dad said it was time to go. I turned to my mum and I sat there knowing....well I just knew. So I held her hand and said goodbye and that was the last time I ever saw her.

My Mum
Gillian Margaret Headington
1942–1989
R.I.P.

What Just Happened

It was a year and twelve days in the space between my brother Robert and my mum`s passing away. It was like a huge whirlwind—first you get sucked in then you get spun out. I was in between getting sucked and spun. Actually the whole thing sucked, but what can you do when you're growing up at that age? Nothing, that's what.

It was like a dream; I didn't think it was real. I thought that my mum and brother were hiding or something and I really wanted them to come back. Something had died inside of me and the more I wanted to pretend it didn't happen, something was telling me to open my eyes and face up to the truth.

On the day my mother died, my father had received a phone call early in the morning. He was requested to go to the hospital in Bristol. As we got there it was me, my dad, and my brother Chris and his wife, Sharon. The doctor had told us to follow him into his office and said "I'm very sorry to inform you that Mrs. Headington passed away in the early hours of this morning." Everyone looked at me and only me, so all attempts to hold back my tears were going to fail miserably. When we got outside I said to my dad, "No, she can't be dead, I know she is hiding, she's got to be hiding." But no matter what I said, nothing was going to bring her back. We left the hospital and were on our way home when I suddenly realised that my dad had to tell my sister and it was not long before her birthday, and I couldn't help thinking, What a present. When we finally got home my father told me to go and get my sister. It was almost like a role reversal from when my sister had gotten me up after my brother had passed away—so I had to get my sister to let her know what she was about to be told. Anyway my sister was in the same position I was in; it wasn't a good situation to be in. My dad said, "Your mum passed away this morning." She looked at us all and I think she knew deep down that this had been going to happen.

I can't remember much of that day or what I go up to. The only thing I didn't want to do was to go out and see anyone; I'd just lost my mum so I didn't feel like socializing. On the day of the funeral I remember going to the toilet just to have a moment to myself and then my dad came in and asked me if I was okay but I just cried and as I did so my dad was not long in shedding a few tears as well. Before we both went out, we composed ourselves for what was going to be another hard day. There weren't very many people at my mother's funeral apart from some of our family and some close friends who turned up to say their last goodbyes.

One thing my mother told me to do was to pray hard for my brother Robert in the hope he would get better but he never did. I thought that if I do the same for my mum then she might get better but she never did. The one thing I know that I shouldn't have done was walking into the bathroom when my mum was sick. With all that blood everywhere I knew that it wasn't something I was going to forget in a hurry but I just wanted to share it with my mum so she wouldn't feel totally alone. One other thing I remember was seeing this book my mum had given me,—the Bible. I started questioning this book: Was there a God? I thought to myself, If there was a God then maybe my mother and brother would still be here. I also had another thought which was completely different: It felt like a huge weight had been lifted off my shoulders. But if I thought that then maybe there was a God and maybe he took them away from me so they wouldn't suffer anymore.

Both my mother's and my brother's ashes were scattered underneath the big tree in the woods that my brother had camped under when he ran away from home. I was asked if I wanted to go that day, but I decided not to as I already said goodbye once before and I didn't feel like saying goodbye a second time.

I returned to school after about a week to forget what just happened. When I got into the classroom, the first topic of conversation was the fact that my mum had passed away. The teacher told all of the other kids in the classroom and it was the same when my brother died. I tried to fight the tears back but I was unable to. A couple of weeks later I was minding my own business when I overheard some of the teachers talking about me so I thought I might just as well listen to see what was so interesting. As I stood there one of them asked who was going to look after me and an other classmate said, "I'll look after Lee." It was one of the best people I've ever known and that person since then has been my best friend and will be forever.

When my sister and I got home, we would always have a bag of crisps and a can of Coke waiting for us. When I saw that these familiar things were no longer live, I knew from that moment on that this was no dream but a disturbing reality.

I knew that this was the last real moment I was ever going to share with my mum. It felt like the last remaining chapter in my life had closed and it was time to start a new one. It was going to be hard but I'd have to adjust—there was no other option.

The Mark of the Devil

When I was growing up there was this game called the weegie board. Well I thought that it was a game, but when I started playing it, I realized that it was no ordinary game—it was something else which my sister was very inquisitive about.

I didn't really know what to think about this game of death I shall call it. As I have come to know, it's not a game you want to take lightly, and if you play with it too much it's going to be hazardous to your health.

I remember when it was the end of a year for the older students. Out with the old, in with the new. We had a big party to celebrate them going off to college or whatever it was they were going to do. My sister and I were staying with my brother and his wife, Sharon, who drove us to the party; they were going to pick us up afterward. I watched as everyone got up and danced but not me; I hated dancing but then I was only fifteen so I wasn't too thrilled about getting up in front of everyone and showing off. All I did all night was sit on a chair and watch the whole evening unfold before me. As I started tilting my chair back I fell all the way back and there wasn't anything I could hold on to, to stop myself from falling, so I just took what was about to happen. Slam! went the chair on the school assembly-hall floor which looked like wood but was actually concrete. I thought I was going to break my neck but to my surprise I was okay. I thought it was the funniest thing ever and upon seeing this my friend came over with his chair and did exactly the same as me. So together we tilted our chairs and we were falling all night which I thought was great. This went on for about half an hour, tilting and falling but I suddenly heard something going on in the hallway so I went out to inspect all the commotion. It was my sister and two of her friends crying and becoming hysterical. I didn't really know what was going on, other than that there was a lot of screaming. All I saw when I walked into the hallway was my sister crying and so were two of her friends. I couldn't understand why but all I heard was that they were playing some game in the girls' toilets and then when it got really heavy they decided to end it. My sister and the two others said that when they did that, they could all feel a burning on the backs of their necks and when one of them tried to open the door to get out there was something wrong with the door—or was there something else in there with them? I'm not a believer in any of that nonsense so I just forgot it.

When playing the weegie board you have a small board and a glass with the alphabet letters cut into squares so they are all separate with yes and no opposite one another. Well a couple of weeks later I asked my sister about what happened that night and she confirmed what I had thought. She told me a little more than I wanted to know. I really wished she would have kept this information to herself instead of telling me. She also told me she was going to die when she reached the age of eighteen. When she told me that, my whole world fell to pieces. Not only did I lose my brother and my mother, I was going to lose my sister as well and it wasn't something I was looking forward to. She was only sixteen at the time so I had to wait a whole two years for that day to come. But there was one thing I didn't do this time, and that was pick up the Bible and start praying. I knew it didn't work, so what would be different this time round?

I had a look at this scar behind my sister's neck—at the time I didn't believe her. It was like a soft red bloody mark with little darker reddish brown spots on it. Something that I had never seen before. Two down, one to go, if I thought that it was true.

I remember when I was back in college and I was doing some fitness exercises in the gym there was one of the girls who was present on the night they were all playing the weegie board. She was a good friend back then and someone I really liked, but there was this other guy who liked her and because we were good friends I don't think he liked it very much. So much so that he wanted to set a gang of bikers onto me for being her friend when he wasn't even going out with her. Anyway, she got to hear about it and went off the deep end at him. After which he left me alone.

Well as I was good friends with this girl, I was play-fighting with her once and when she turned her back I noticed something on the back off her neck—it was the same mark my sister has on her neck. I looked again and I didn't know what to think. One thought that did go through my mind was two down, one to go.

When I lived in a town that was the same place I went to, I thought to myself, I didn't really see this other girl about too much so if I did then I was going to have to walk up to her and ask if I could see the back of her neck. This is not something I do every day so she might have thought I was being weird or something, but I knew she liked going to the pubs and clubs so I thought it might have been better if I bumped into her then.

Well a few years on and I had my chance. I was in a club with a friend and I was on the dance floor and I saw her dancing with some of her friends so I danced closer to her but as I was a rubbish dancer I thought this was an impossibility so I just danced in one spot. I thought I was going to miss my chance and it so happened that an ex-wife of another friend of mine was there and she spotted me and danced over to say hi and that was when I could see this girl more closely. I thought as she danced over I could engage her in conversation. So I got chatting with her—I knew her, as we went to the same school together. As we were chatting I mentioned that night to her. The night at this dance for me was a bit of a blur but I do however remember asking to see the back of her neck, which she didn't seem to mind. She lifted her hair up and that was when I saw the same scar on the back of her neck. So that was it—all three were telling the truth.

One thing I will say is that when I hear about UFOs flying in our skies and people seeing them, I'm not too sure if they are telling the truth. But this I did believe. I saw three scars, so how much more proof did I need? They were all there that night and all had the same story and all had the same scar. It takes a lot for me to believe in things that are unexplainable, but this well, I'll let you be the judge of this one, but I think there are some dark forces at work.

I'll Take Two but I'll Give You Seven

When everything happened to the family, I wasn't able to understand what was going on. I guess I was too young to grasp the fact that I had lost my brother to cancer and a year and twelve days afterward I lost my mum. I felt something, but I was unsure of what that feeling was.

When my father came back to live, I think he wanted to get his head down and just get on with things. As a family with only three of us living in a three-bedroom semi-detached house, there was a lot to do. The garden was a mess, so was the house. All of the rubbish we had went into the two giant holes we had in the back of our garden. All of my mother's and brother's belongings went to the local charity shop. I felt that things were moving at a rate that I didn't want them to. These were the only things that related to the past and I didn't want to part with them. If you could imagine that you're a child and you're next to the one thing that you cherish the most and someone comes over, picks you up, and walks you further and further away from it all, and you put your arms over the person's shoulder for the past to come and rescue you—well that is exactly what I wanted. Everything that was happening at that moment was for the best—I can see that now that I am looking back on them.

Things gradually returned to the norm but if I thought they were going to get a lot easier, then I was again mistaken.

I remember when my dad called me into the front room. He was sitting there with this lady that I've come to know so well now. "Lee, this is Stella. Stella, this is my youngest son, Lee." "Hello," I said, and she said the same to me. The first thing I started to think was, "I've seen her before," so as I left them alone and walked out into the living room, I started to think about where it was that I'd seen her but for the love of me, I couldn't think of where.

Anyway, the morning after I asked my dad where it was that I'd seen her before and he said the Village Club, "Oh, yeah," I said. I was glad for my dad—he finally found someone he liked very much and it's safe to say that she liked him too. I remember that the first time she came up for Sunday lunch and sat next to me I felt a little honored. When I was eating my dinner I would pause to look at her eating her dinner and she kept raising her shoulders as if to say she was really enjoying her lunch and the fact that she came round. When we got to know her more she gradually began to move in some of her stuff. She also bought a factory home with her—endless cards. My sister and I used to help her with them. One card, one slip of paper, into a plastic sleeve, and then came the sticker. We all must have done that over a million times. I didn't mind as I was in college and I didn't really do anything else with my time. Living with my dad was a good thing and helping out around the house kept me from hanging around with the people I usually hung out with. While they all had their own curricular activities like taking drugs, the basis of that practice's appeal really didn't get me excited much.

When my dad's new girlfriend finally moved in with us we got to meet all of her family. She has a daughter who was and still is a pleasant individual. She also has a son, who is also a very outstanding guy and is married with three sons. It was hard for me to move on from where I had originally come from and accept that life goes on. When we got to know her family, we got to know that they too didn't have much of a run of good luck, so I guess we all had something in common. They weren't a family that grew up with golden spoons in their mouths, which I would have felt intimidated by. We came to understand that my father's new girlfriend had been through the mill by all of the other men she had previous relationships with. Naturally, my dad's kind gestures she found hard to understand, as all the other men had used her for a punching bag.

She left on some occasions, which my dad, sister, brother, and myself found hard to deal with. We were an understanding family and as the saying goes, "Rome wasn't built in a day." My sister had been going through some personal problems and as a result of that she made life difficult at home for my dad's new girlfriend and so Stella moved out, which I didn't really feel was the right decision but since she knew a lot of people in the town I was going to move to, I guess it was better all round. I myself could have given her a hard time when she left for the last time, but I knew that she and my father needed each other and if I did give her a hard time then my father would have never forgiven me. But who was I to stand in the way of true love? And it wasn't in my nature to be nasty to the ones I love so I just left them to work on their relationship.

I have no regrets about meeting Stella's family and I never will. We all have our faults but we wouldn't be human if we didn't. Our family lost two family members but we gained an additional six, including Stella and they are a family we have all come to appreciate so much.

That Dark Road

I knew there were dark paths around everywhere but I didn't think for one minute that I would go down one. I have been a great lover of watching suspense and action films, even when about guns or drugs. I thought those things never really intruded everyday living but I guess I was wrong. When Robert died, his best mate told me that if he ever found out that I was going down that road he would kick my ass from here to there and back. He wasn't someone I really wanted to get on the wrong side of at the age I was at that time so I said I would never go near things like that. If I thought for one minute he would be the one who was going to be my partner in experimenting with these things I never would have believed it.

When I was living at home, my dad kept me from hanging round with the wrong crowd and of course they never liked me much in Yatton anyway so I think they all did me a favor. It was a different story when I moved out and was made redundant from my job. I moved into the worst place possible. Things were good at the start. Got to meet a few people, make friends, and hang out, which is what I enjoyed. There were some other people in there I would have liked to avoid. I just was more interested in making friends and whatever they did wrong I didn't see the harm in it, but I knew the things they were doing were wrong but it wasn't my business to say if they were right or wrong because I knew they would have given me a load of verbal for my trouble anyway, so I just went along with whatever they did and kept my mouth shut.

I remember one night when this girl was out for about a week and two other residents decided it would be a good idea to break into her flat. The doors to the flats were really flimsy so they were easy to kick through. That was my first taste of what was to come. Some of the violence I saw was something I never wanted to see for the rest of my life. There was this one guy who licked his knife before he was going to put it through a girl's stomach. People's flats were getting broken into. I got to know a lot about drugs, tenths, eighths, quarters, the list goes on and on. I remember when I wanted to find out what the fuss was all about so I bought a tenth off one of the other residents who had started dealing. So that night I tried a little contraption called a bucket. Basically you have a bucket filled with water, an empty plastic bottle, and something to put on top of the bottle top to filter the tobacco and whatever drug you decided to put with the tobacco, light the top, bring the bottle up as it fills with smoke, and then take the top off and put your mouth over the top and suck and push down at the same time. So there I was about to do my first one. Before I did I drank a small bottle of vodka, so I was feeling a bit drunk at the start of it. Anyway I did the bucket and sat down. Ten minutes into it, my whole body just went numb and I filled with pins and needles. I was feeling so out of my head I decided to crawl back to my flat. I felt that I wasn't moving that fast so I got to my feet but as I was about to walk, I felt like someone had pushed me from behind so they could hurry me on my merry way. As I got to my door I stopped and passed out. I didn't feel much when my head hit the floor, but I did remember telling myself to get up before anyone saw me laying there. I got into my flat and just went to bed. I was so ill I had to rush to the bathroom and was sick a few times. Some of the girls who were living there at the time banged on my door but couldn't get a reply as I felt drained of all my energy. That was an experience I was happy to leave behind.

I had done this sort of thing in the past but not to that extent. Every time I did this though I felt dirty and cheap. I started smoking, the drinking got more heavy. I did things to people which I'm not proud of. I felt that I was nothing at that point. I felt like a scum-sucking little worm and I couldn't bear to look at myself in the mirror. I hated myself for letting this happen to me and I still do. All the money I got from the dole centre I spent it on alcohol. I had parties that were organized by other people. I had someone from the same building as me living with me. He used to invite people I didn't know back to my flat but I didn't feel like it was mine anymore. I started to get a bad reputation because of everything that happened there. I should have stopped it but I didn't.

I felt alone. As much as I had people who were my friends at the time around me, I still felt isolated.

I moved out into my sister's to start afresh but I got made redundant so I had to move out. I managed to find myself a small bedsit but that got broken into by my next-door neighbour. I felt violated, so I decided to move again, only this time it was above a pub which was really dingy. The shower was in the same room as my bedroom and my kitchen. When the landlord had new windows put in the building, some of my belongings went missing when they came to do my bedsit so I told the landlord but he told me to stop being an idiot. This started to get up my nose so I did a midnight split from there too and moved to another location.

This time it was going to be different. I started to enjoy living in my next bedsit. I had found myself another job which was only just down the road so it was convenient. I got put on a lot by this next job but I enjoyed working there and did so for the next six years. A lot of things happened in those six years. I lost my brother Chris, someone I thought was really close to me and I felt would never make me feel small, but was I wrong. This made me question friendships with people I thought would never hurt me. This has taught me a very tough lesson. Even with blood... but that is a situation best left there.

As my sister was going through all the bad things in her life, she had three kids to bring up and I didn't really feel that she had a happy life doing so. She started to take medication for what I think was depression at the time but I was told that there were sinister goings-on in the house she was living in. There was one point where she was committed to a mental hospital. If I thought it would have done any good, I would have tried to talk her out of it but I felt powerless to do anything for her. I knew deep down this wasn't what my sister wanted in her life. This was like a raging fire, it was getting worse. She kept trying to take her own life. I went round one night when she was in bed and when she came down to see me she was as thin as a rake and I just knew it was only a matter of time. It also got to the stage where I was tired and fed up—that I wished she would succeed. Buy mostly I felt sorry for her. I just wanted to take her away and for her to get better but I also knew deep down she would have given me hell if I tried to do so.

One day at work, I was working on a slab press and all of a sudden I started to think about all the good and bad things in my life. So I stood there and thought, "What have I really got going for me? A dead-end job, no girlfriend, I live on my own, and everyone had left me,"— so I thought, Fuck it, I'm going to end it tonight. I shocked myself by what I had decided, but I'd had enough and couldn't take anymore and it wasn't worth carrying on. It was time for my dinner so I thought I would go and join my dad. We engaged in conversation about what we thought was going to happen with my sister. Tears rolled down his eyes and he said, "How can she just want to keep trying to take her life?" Other people came in for their dinner, and my dad just wanted to forget about it. Nothing was said from there on in. I thought I couldn't leave my dad at this point—if I killed myself, it would have killed him. So as for the suicidal thought I had earlier, I just left it where it was for the time being.

Things started to go from bad to worse. I felt I was getting more and more depressed and was taking time off because of it. My sister's ex-husband was treating his kids like dirt. Social services weren't doing enough. I decided to get involved as did my parents. I made myself ill because of this whole situation. I got so wound up, I felt a deep pounding in my chest and this didn't feel good so I tried to ignore it. It felt like a small heart attack so I tried to calm myself down before the real thing did happen. I started hating myself even more. I was in a boring job. I tried to keep my mind occupied so I joined a gym which I went to for three years as well as going to college for the same amount of time. Although I knew the inevitable was going to happen I stuck my head in the sand and I didn't face things head on as I should have done.

When I moved back home to be with my stepmum and dad, I thought things were looking up, some of the time I've spent there was good but it wasn't going to last forever. One night I was sitting in the pub with my mum and dad. I told them I was really unhappy, so they told me, if I really wanted to leave the job I was in then I should do it. Little did they know that I already had typed my notice out.

My mood progressively got worse as I sunk deeper into depression. I went to see a counselor seven miles from where I lived for a few months. I felt like I was turning a corner in my life and I even told myself so. I wanted to believe it so much I tried to convince myself of that. When I finished with the counselor, I felt like I lost my rock. When I talked to her I felt like moss growing on the edge of an ocean rock. I was there to build myself upon this rock I called my counselor. That wasn't to last as she left to help other people in different parts of the world. One month on and I felt like I was back where I started. Talking helps, bringing back up the things that have happened to you from the past that you want to forget is like picking at a scab that has healed already. I should have known then not to bring all this to the surface. I went for a walk to the top of the woods to a small bench to regroup but all I really wanted to do was to disappear. The thoughts that were going through my mind were very dark. I asked myself something that day. "Is this all that's left?"

My Pure Evil Hatred

I don't quite understand where my feelings of hatred come from. When I was growing up, I never would have thought I would be capable of feeling the way that I do. Is it me? Did I do something wrong in life? Well I don't know and I'm really fed up with feeling this way. But it does start somewhere.

If I look back and see where my hatred started from then I think its safe to say it began when I got bullied in school and if that wasn't enough I had it at home as well. I'm not sure how many people it takes to bully others but I got it from eleven people in my class. I'll never know to this day exactly why they all bullied me, it's just another one of those unanswered questions. If I saw any of the people who bullied me from my past I don't even think I can be bothered to ask them. They are all worthless and I hope they all meet a grizzly end to their whole sorry lives. I also got bullied from my own family members. I was the youngest of my family so maybe that is why I had to take all the heartache that I did. I've taken a lot of hassle to put it lightly from quite a few people. When I got bullied at school, I recall one day when I was walking into the school gates and there were a few others that I wouldn't care to mention, and when I walked up to them I said morning to them all and then one of them held my arms behind my back and another started to lay into me. I was hit so hard I don't even know what started it all.

At my secondary school I got bullied there too. It was normal to see a chair flying past my head. Although I got bullied at my junior school and those days will always be with me 'til the day I die, secondary school wasn't all that bad. My sister had softened the blow because she went there first so most of the tough boys left me alone well at least for a while. The one thing I can say is that I made a few good friends from that school, which I'll never regret. Next, came college.

I attended the college of further education for two years which went seemingly well. I never really wanted to be there half the time but as I lost my mother and brother I needed something to take my mind off things. But as tough as it was, I never really concentrated and my mind was still in total denial to what had recently happened in my life. One evening when I was walking to the bus stop with a friend of mine, I was sitting on a step outside of a club which was on the main high street. I was looking for the bus but I noticed someone sitting on the wall so I had a bit of a job to see if the bus was coming in. Well as I was waiting for the bus someone shouted something out of a moving car blah blah blah. I couldn't make out any of it, so I just ignored it as anyone else would. The next thing I know is that I'm getting called all the names under the sun but there was one name that stood out the most: "prick." This was this guy's favorite word. Whenever he saw me that's all he ever called me. I didn't even know why. I thought that he might just get tired of it as I never used to say anything back to him— but no, he carried on as normal, prick this and prick that. I wanted to confront this guy but I was scared and there was no getting around the fact that I was a bit of a weakling. I just knew he was going to hit me— and what for? I was only looking for the bus.

Well one night when I was with a friend of mine, I was sitting in a bus shelter on a sea front when I saw this black car pull up and this guy got out and from that moment I knew I was in trouble but I also knew that if I ran or walked away it would fester even longer so I just sat there and waited for what was about to happen. He walked up and said, "You called me a fuckin' prick, didn't you?" "No," I said back. So I thought Here we go but he's on his own so things can't be that bad. Well they were about to get worse when four of his mates joined him so I had no hope and neither did my friend. The one thing that I will always remember about that night is there was this girl; who was with this guy, she kept pulling my hair. What could I do apart from sit there and take it all? I knew that if I fought back I would get a right pummeling. When they finally had enough the guy who was after me punched me in the side of my face, stood over me, then left. My friend said, "Lee, are you okay? I'm going to get the police" So I said, "No, I'm all right, just don't leave," as I thought they were going to come back for a second helping. Anyway, they didn't and I stayed at this hotel where my friend was staying, and then I left in the morning.

After that I had a bit of a drinking problem and I had a chip on my shoulder. I felt like everyone had it in for me for some unknown reason. I didn't want to think about it too much. I just drank every time I thought about it. One time when I went out to a club, I was involved in a bit of a ruckus. I and three of my friends were sitting on a four-seater bench and these two blokes came up and told us all to get out, so one of my friends moved and I thought the same thing. So I tried to move but this guy wouldn't let me out and the next thing I know I get a headbutt from the left and three punches to the face from the front so I forced my way out. The funny thing is that one of the guys I was with said he wouldn't let anyone beat us all up—what a joke that was. I felt something boil inside me, a real quick feeling of anger. I just went home to forget the whole thing.

Having a girlfriend has its problems, especially one known by half of the town I was hanging around in. One guy got really upset with me because I was seeing his ex-girlfriend. Well that's not my fault—maybe if you treated her with a bit more respect then you might have still been with her. This guy had such a problem with this he got half of the town of boy racers on my back. What a total moron, if he can't come to me and tell me to my face and he has to get a mob of at least thirty people do it for him. A total loser. I'm less trusting toward people that I don't know because of the way things have gone in my life.

A couple of years went by and I've got a nice place to live and I have myself a good job, or so I thought. I worked at a warehouse fork-lift driving and picking up orders. All I wanted to do was to get my head down and get on with it but no, the owner had a rather large chip on his shoulder and every time he went abroad to buy his stock I breathed a sigh of relief. It was a different story when he came back though. I would arrive for work in the morning and get on with what I do best when I'd turn the corner he's walking down the warehouse. "Fuck," I say to myself and when he is about to pass me I would wait for him to say something, and here it is: "Lee, what are doing Saturday?" "Nothing," I say back. "Can you work?"—and just to keep the peace I would say okay and he would walk off and not even say thank you. This happened quite a few times; there wasn't a moment's peace, he just wanted to come down and help out but I really think he only did it because he was bored. Another time that he asked me to work a Saturday he had asked someone else who worked in the ware-house. I saw this other guy walk out of the office muttering something to himself and walking off upset with himself for agreeing to work a Saturday when he wished he hadn't. I thought to myself that I had to say something or he would never leave me alone. So one Friday afternoon I was picking up an order he was in the same place where I had to get the box I wanted, so I waited for the question, and of course it came: "Lee, now that you've seen your doctor, your dentist, your financial adviser, and your father, what are you doing Saturday?" I'd run out of excuses but I really didn't feel like working Saturday, and this owner didn't respect me much anyway so I said, "I'm going to the hair dressers." "So you can't work?" "No," I said. "you're fuckin' useless." "Yep, I said back, so off I went on my merry way feeling really proud of myself—for all the times that guy had had a go at me and called me names, I got my own back. Well he didn't speak to me for three months but I didn't care much; I didn't like him anyway.

I left there and I went to work somewhere else. But if I thought I was going to have an easy ride there then I was mistaken again and it was going to be worse. It first started quietly, just getting on with things, and the others were really helpful.

Anyway there was this other person who came to work there and all he did was throw his weight about everywhere, and one week this resulted in the whole warehouse giving me the silent treatment. I just ignored it and on that Friday evening I went to one of the office staff who was in charge and told him I wouldn't be there on Monday morning. He tried to talk me out of it but I was really unhappy there and to this day wished I'd never gone back. On that Monday two of them came round to my bedsit and asked me to come back and I unwillingly said yes. It was going to be the biggest mistake of my life. This guy in question was always throwing pieces of wood at me and slamming me into walls and taking the piss out of me. What was I going to do? I couldn't tell the manager because it would have seemed like I was a grass so I was stuck. One afternoon I was putting away wood when he was serving a customer and he asked me to go and get something for his customer. When I told him to do it himself, well he wasn't having that and threw a twenty-five foot piece of wood at me, which hit me a fraction above my temple. I wished that it had fuckin' killed me—then I would be better off.

To this day it winds me up and I wished that I'd done something about it. I'm angry with myself for that and only I can live with it.

Another place I worked at gradually got to me in the end. When I first went to work there I really enjoyed it but I thought it was something I was going to have to get used to. Well when one person left, another had to take his place and do all the demeaning jobs. I worked there for six years walking around picking up rubbish which is what I hated doing. Some of the things they got me to do were okay and they gave me a lot of time off but there were also things happening in my family making for an unstoppable force of problems I was unable to cope with.

My brother was killing himself and it wasn't fast but really slow and the worse thing is that I couldn't stop him, he just didn't want to know anymore and to top that his ex-wife took everything, and had affairs with different blokes, but the worst thing is that she wanted his money. So all this just fed my anger even further. It just took it to a whole new level.

For some reason every time I watch England play football, I only watch them to see them lose. I hate England to the very core. I feel like it has done nothing for me and if we were ever to get into a war and they needed everyone, I would turn my back on it. When my dad had a heart attack this government never helped my family. When both my brothers died and my mother died, where were they to say they were sorry to hear about that? They do so to some families, so why not mine? I hate driving every day and dislike other road users—how can some people be so completely stupid? I often wonder where they get their drivers' licenses—the internet? I hate the fact that when I see some who I hate they deserve everything they get. I just wanna jump on their heads until they get brain damage. I hate the fact that some people have had a go at my family and I can't have a go back at them for it you know who you are! Some people who treat others badly get all the luck in the world. Well I hope your luck runs out!

Forever My Saviour

As a result of my being bullied all the time I found myself afraid of being a weakling for the rest of my life. I had nobody to teach me how to defend myself apart from my brother Chris who taught me how to punch for about half an hour. I had a lot of friends also but none of them ever helped me. After the death of my brother, everyone seemed to gang up on me. There was one person who kept trying to set me up as well, trying to get me to fight some of the other kids in our neighbourhood. But the thing was, he was supposed to be one of my friends. I listened to a lot of music when I was growing up but there was no music I could listen to that related to my situation. There were people like Michael Jackson, Erasure, M.C. Hammer, East 17, Take-That, and Boy George. Whenever I listened to them, I had to turn off the radio in a hurry. When this type of music was on, I associated it to the bullying I was receiving, so every time I listen to it now and again I go back to the days when this kept happening to me. I think this is why I hate all the older bands now. I just couldn't care less if they dropped off the face of the planet.

From the 1990s to 2000 all there were was disco, trance, so-called rock, and rn'b. All of which I couldn't decide about listening to. The music I needed was on the way. I feel now that it's late coming about, the damage has been done and sometimes I feel like smashing to pieces all the music I now listen to. But I suppose it's better late than never. All the beatings I took and never fought back about will be with me forever. I hate myself for never having a go back and show them I wasn't a complete loser.

I see this music as my saviour and nothing else. My father is my saviour and so is the best mother in the world, whose name happens to be Stella. With those two by my side I don't fear anything.

When I was going through my personal journey, I never had the things I wanted to support me. Okay I had my family but not all the time. The longer I was living on my own the more I sought solace in my own company. I became a recluse. I didn't want anyone else near me. When I came to be this way, it was an easy routine to get into but an even harder one to get out of. When I lived in the sixth place in this town, I became even worse. My family wanted me to come home for dinner and to spend some time with them but all I wanted to was be on my own. When I did spend the day and night with them, all I looked forward to was coming home, back to my flat. The more this happened the more I felt like I was walking a dark path, but I wasn't sure where it was going to take me.

I had a major disagreement with some people which resulted in me not talking to them for two years or more. They were also involved with my mum and dad. I knew that it was a situation best left alone for the time being. If I made the decision to be in the same room with them when they were staying with my mum and dad then it would have only resulted in us all having a huge argument. The whole reason why I didn't talk to them for two years was to teach them a very tough lesson. I know for a fact now that they will think twice before they attempt to upset me now. I feel that they are better people now. It is something I have watched and they will always have me in their corner for all eternity and I wouldn't want it any other way.

As for music, I also started listening to this "new metal," as they called it. This was like no other music for me. It was like I had finally found a part of myself that I had been lacking in my life. These bands were hard, aggressive, violent, and emotional but I liked it. This music was like a shield, I felt nothing could penetrate me. It was my guardian angel. The band that I related to the most and which brought out the beast in me was Limp Bizkit and I will be forever thankful to them. More bands playing this kind of music followed. It gave me confidence to do things I would normally shy away from. The words of the songs gave me goose pimples, along with the beating of the drums and the strumming of the guitars. Every time I listened to the climax to every song and the musicians gave it their all, I just wanted to beat my head and fists to be included to the music, but as it finished I also just wanted to collapse on the floor and cry my eyes out. This music touched me. Every time I got up for work I listened to a couple of tracks before I was due to start and when I got home, I listened to the whole album of the artist I was interested in at the time. I will enjoy this music for the rest of my life, not only because it helped me but because it saved me. I feel like I owe this music my life.

Chris

Every time I hear the name Chris I will always think of my oldest brother and his saying "He's sound as a pound," words I will always remember him for.

Most people have their bad points and if my brother had any they were very few. He appreciated everything. Music, humour, pool, and he loved a pack of baccie and a pint of cider in his hand. All of these he enjoyed in the company of his friends. When my brother lived at home I rarely saw him. When he was home he was asleep for most of the day or else working to fund his next party or visit to a status-quo gig. My brother was a lover not a fighter.

I remember when I, my sister, and my mum went to see my dad at his workplace. As we did, we walked past Chris's place of work and I saw him having a game of cricket with his work friends. We all stopped to watch him play and as we did so he looked behind as if he sensed us being there and he waved at us all, so we all waved back. I'll never forget that day for as long as I live.

When my brother moved out, he got into a relationship with his first love, with whom he fathered a baby boy. I also remember when my mother and I went round to visit my brother's girlfriend and his son. The thing I most remember was the time I had a plastic green grasshopper and I let his baby son play with it while we were there; but I had to take it with me when we left because he thought it was his breakfast. I can't really remember why, but the relationship ended for reasons unknown. It will always remain another one of those questions unanswered, but I think it's better left that way. My brother wasn't the one to let everyone know about his business.

About a couple of months later he'd found himself a new girlfriend whom he brought home so all the family could meet her. Even some of my brother Robert's friends were there and little did Chris know that all of them were making fun of what she looked like. All I remember was her blonde curly hair and her big wide smile. My brother was happy enough—he moved twelve miles away to be with her. I'm not entirely sure on how long they were together before they got married but it was going to be a very eventful day.

I heard a rumour that this girl's brother had cornered Chris and threatened him saying if he were ever to hurt his sister he would kill him. What a thing to hear someone say just as you are about to marry the woman you are going to spend the rest of your life with! I also re-member a time when I was fishing with my dad and my brother came to see how we were getting on—or so I thought. But my brother was in tears, terrified for his life. I would have loved to know why.

When I look back at the relationship of my brother and his wife, I thought it was good from the start. They had some really fun times and I wished I was with them more. One evening my brother and his wife came round to tell us all that there was a new addition to the family. My father, my new mum, and myself were all happy for them, none more so than my brother who had already fathered a son with his first love but was never able to see him. But I think this all made up for that.

Some years later Chris's second son was born. When we found that out, there was a knock at the door which happened to be my brother—he stepped in and said, "All right, Unc." I thought he had "All right, hunk," said, so I said, "Oh, what do you mean?" "You're going to be an uncle for a second time." "Oh," I said. I was pleased for him and his wife and the fact that there was going to be another addition to the family. Everything was going just right for them and deservedly so.

When I moved out for the first time in my life, I moved to the same town as my brother. Although we were living in the same place we didn't really visit each other very much, but every time we did we more then made up for it. He had a local near his house so he didn't really have too far to walk—which was good because I would have to walk a couple of miles just to see him and the buses weren't all that trusting so I thought it would be better to walk instead.

A few months had passed and I still thought that everything was going okay that was, until I got a phone call saying that Chris had done a disappearing act. Upon hearing this I instantly got worried for my brother, not knowing where he was or if he was okay. After a week he returned home back to his wife and kids so I thought he might need a brotherly ear to talk things over but when I got there his wife was present and she wouldn't leave the room so we had to find something else to talk about. For some reason, my brother running away was something I couldn't understand because he would never tell any of his family about it. I wished he had confided in me.

When I did go and visit him we would sit there and have a laugh and as soon as his wife would hear something she didn't like then all hell would jump out of her mouth and she would belittle my brother—and it wasn't something I liked to listen to.

Because of what was going on, Chris turned to drink a lot more than usual. I would phone him up but his wife would answer instead. He was either tired or he had a bottle of cider. Things weren't going well at home and I think she gave him a hard time. She says it was because of his drinking habits that she couldn't live with it anymore but since she kept belittling him all the time I'm sure that's why he'd had enough. What made things worse was when he slipped two discs in his back and in the end they crumbled so he was at home most of the time. He could lift anything before, but now and the only thing he could pick up was his kids from school.

Soon, Chris's wife came up to the house and cried her eyes out and told my dad and my stepmum that would they have a problem if she kicked him out as he was drinking all the time. The reply wasn't in favour of keeping my brother in the house he provided for his family. After this my brother did another disappearing act, but this time it was for about a month. I was told where he was living but I didn't know the number so I got on my mountain bike to see if I could find out which house it was. Little did I know it was a bedsit. My brother reduced to living in a bedsit!

After he moved out, his wife began going out and socializing with different men. One of which was my ex-brother-in-law. He fixed her television and then he got text messages on his phone from her telling him she wanted to pay him in kind; he received seven text messages a day which were of a sexual nature. She also tried it with his brother and I heard a story that they had a kiss, but I'm sure that a lot more happened than just a kiss because she tried it with me. I was drunk one night when my sister was in a bad way. At one point I thought I was going to lose my sister—I thought she was going to die with all the medication she was taking. So one night when I was really distraught, my brother's wife phoned me and asked to see me to make sure I was okay it was going to be the worst mistake of my life. When we were chatting and she was about to leave, she said," I don't see you as Chris's little brother anymore." I didn't really know what to think or say apart from thank you—what else could I say. But before she left she asked if she could kiss me goodbye, I said yes, and before I knew it I was full on kissing her. This was wrong of me and deep down I knew it but I wasn't in a good frame of mind that night, so I guess the only thing I could put that experience down to was me being upset and vulnerable. The next morning it didn't take me long to wise up and feel like I'd done the dirty on my brother. I just wanted to forget the whole episode. The other thing I couldn't help thinking was that if she could do this to my brother and then move on to my ex-brother-in-law and then two others, then did she really love my brother like she said she did? When I went to see my brother I thought about telling him but I knew that if I did he would never forgive me and never talk to me again. He already felt like he didn't have anyone else, so I thought that it wouldn't be a good idea telling him as he would never forgive me and never talk to me again. Such a small thing, I didn't want to lose him over.

When he was living in this gritty little bedsit he took a turn for the worse. When he learned that his wife had found someone else, that crushed him. As he was still drinking and smoking, I now know that this was his only escape from everything he loved and lost. When I went round one evening, his two sons where there, just about to leave, but just before they did, one of his sons started coughing, desperate for his father to see him doing so, since he wanted his dad to quit smoking. As I saw this I looked at him and then I saw myself when my mum was doing the same. I felt so sorry for him. I knew he was going to be without a father soon, but whether he knew or not, that was something I was unaware of. I felt powerless to do anything while my brother was inching his way slowly towards death. When he got information from his wife that she wanted a divorce, he told me the very same night. I asked him how he felt about this situation. He said, "I don't want a divorce but if she wants one, there isn't much I can do I'm afraid." "Well, no," I replied.

Chris had to go to Newport in Wales to have a back examination so they could determine whether or not he was fit for work. This happened quite a number of times which I think was unfair as there are a lot of people out there giving their sob stories about how bad their backs are and my brother had genuinely crippled his back. The place where he worked was under a pending claim for compensation for my brother's ill health but they wouldn't accept liability, which I also happen to think was unfair. When we got to Newport all my brother wanted to do was to find the nearest pub but I said to him that we should find this back hospital first so we would know where we were going. "Good idea," he said to me. Anyway, we found the hospital so now we could find a pub. The nearest one was burnt down and this absolutely ticked my brother. Come all the way to Wales and the nearest pub was burned to a crisp. We walked on and found another pub. When we got there, my brother ordered a vodka and lime and I had a cup of coffee. There was a pool table so my brother and I had a couple of games. After this we sat down and had a chat. I can't remember half of what we were talking about; I just loved being there and spending some time with him. When we got to the hospital we sat down, and then my brother turned to me and said, "Don't worry, Lee, my back will get better." When the doctor called him in, I sat there alone and I had a little cry to myself but I had to quickly compose myself because I didn't want to let my brother see that I was upset, so I wiped the tears away and got on with the rest of the day. When we got back to the town we both lived in my brother walked home and so did I after he said thank you for the time we spent together. This was a day I really enjoyed and was never going to forget for the rest of my life.

After a week I went to visit my brother. We got chatting again as there was nothing else to do; I asked how the divorce was going. He said he didn't know, and I asked what he meant. "Well, I got in touch with my solicitor but her solicitor hasn't replied, so I'm assuming she doesn't want a divorce." I started to think about this and suddenly realized that as my brother's health got worse, she thought that if she stayed married to him then she would get his settlement money for crippling his back. Eighteen thousand pounds he got for his trouble. It all made perfect sense. "The money from my will, I want you to look after that," he said. When I asked why, he replied, "Because you're the only one I trust." It was pretty obvious that he didn't trust his wife!

One Saturday afternoon I and my brother were going to meet my dad and stepmum for coffee. When we all decided what we wanted my dad and mum went up to pay for it. When I turned to my brother and asked if he was okay, he looked at me and said, "Lee, I don't know if you will understand this but I'm fed up with getting up, I'm fed up with making myself a cup of coffee, I'm fed up with making myself a piece of toast when it's just as easy to go down to the pub and have a pint. I'm fed up." As my mum and dad walked to our table, my brother wiped away his tears and quickly composed himself before they could see.

When he told me that, I knew he just wanted to go.

A couple of months later when he was taken into hospital and was put on a drip, and he started to get better. He was unhappy and so he discharged himself and wanted to go back to his bedsit to spend the remaining time he had left on his own. When he finally got back, my father and I were waiting for him. He had his wife and our mum with him. When he came through the door, he held out his hand for me to help him and that is something I will always remember. When he got into bed, we had a little bit of a disagreement and it ended with me leaving in a bit of a foul mood. Through the week I pondered whether to go and see him, but I never did and I will regret that for the rest of my life.

The following Saturday I had a phone call from my dad. He asked me whether I was at work so I said that I was. He came in and told me that my brother had passed away, but I already knew deep down. He let out a few tears and so I consoled him as he did so. When I finished work I had a bath and spent the rest of the day with my dad and mum. I didn't grieve in the same way I did when my other brother and my mother had passed away. I was a lot older and wiser so it was going to take more time. Through the coming week my brother's wife phoned me up and said that she and her sons wanted her new fiancé to be at the funeral but I said I didn't want him there out of respect for my brother. She didn't like the reply I gave her so she said, "If my boys want him there then they shall have him there." "No matter what I say you are just going to go ahead and do whatever you want anyway so there's no point in having this conversation anyway," I said, slam, went the phone. All she did that week was throw her weight about, but it wasn't going to go down well with my brother's side of the family. On the day of the funeral I couldn't cry; his wife was there and letting out all the tears for everyone to hear. I felt that she made a mockery of the whole time I was there. That day I had a bit of a scuffle with my sister's ex-husband and I left the pub in a bit of a temper after having an argument with my sister. When I got back to where I was living I drowned my sorrows and I thought I would put together a nasty text and send it to my brother's widow. When she finally read it, all hell broke loose. I had her family try and phone me up but I didn't answer as I knew this would aggravate them further. Instead they phoned my mum and gave her a load of verbal but my mum being the strong argumentative type wasn't going to take any nonsense from anyone, as she had just lost a son as well, so she gave as good as she got.

Two weeks later I went out for a drink with a friend of mine from work—and who happened to be in the same pub as me but her! As she put her hands in the air to celebrate her hen night, there was a copper there she was chatting up. I couldn't help thinking,. Oh yeah, you're really upset about losing your husband aren't you? My friend took one look at my face and said, "Please don't start anything," so out of respect for my friend, I didn't do anything. All I wanted to do was to go over and tip a pint of lager over her head and say," This is one, Chris, congratulations," and walk out. What was all that crying for on the day of the funeral? Crocodile tears, that's what they were.

The following Monday when I got to work I was walking around the site when I just started thinking about my brother and then I just couldn't hold back and I burst into tears, so the manager let me have the rest of the day off. I got home and I listened to a few tracks of my music. As I had all my different tracks all lay out in front of me, I listened to one track, Blink 182's "I Miss You." This was my brother's song as far as I was concerned. I listened to this track all day and I sobbed my heart out for my brother

There was one thing he wished for and that was to say he was sorry for the argument we had when I left that night. I regret not making his wish come true. I phoned a friend that night and I told her every time I listened to this track I kept getting goose pimples. She told me that it might be my brother telling me that he was okay and that he found peace and he was finally at rest.

For about two weeks I just moped around at work. I suppose it didn't really sink in that I had just lost my last brother. One morning at eleven o'clock, Joe Whiley was doing this pet sound on Radio One, where some of the people in England are talking about their lives and how things went wrong for them. There was one person who was talking about his brother and how he had helped him through a rough patch in his life. He said if it wasn't for his brother then he probably would have not been here today and dedicated a song to him. At that stage I said to myself, "I don't have any brothers to do any of that for me now," and I started to become tearful then and only then did I realize my brother wasn't coming back and that he'd gone for good.

I love you, bruv, and I know we will meet again some day. I love you, Chris, and until then, I'll see you soon.

My Brother
Christopher Leslie Headington
1963–2004
R.I.P

Australia

It was a major accomplishment to travel to Australia. My first time on an aeroplane. There were not too many people who had done what I did. Most other people would have traveled somewhere closer just to see if they could put up with wanting to go that far. Spain, France, Italy, or Ireland are normal places people like to travel to first. I'm not one to do things by halves; I like to go whole hog. It took twelve hours to get to Japan first and I stayed there for six hours during the day. It took a further eight hours to get to Sidney but we had to stop over in Brisbane first to fuel up for the final part of the journey. I was so glad when we touched down in Sidney—it had been a bit of a white-knuckle ride from London to Japan. At Sidney airport, I was met by my Uncle Fred and my Auntie Linda with whom I was going to stay for about a month—which is what I, my dad, and my mum arranged to do before I came over. I was greeted with a big hug and a smile by both of them and I was so grateful to them for allowing me to stay in their home. The only thing that came to my mind when we got outside was that I hoped Australia would suck so I wouldn't fall off. Well, I *was* on the bottom part of the planet, after all.

I was pleased the traveling was over but I did have another hour-and-a-half drive back to my uncle and auntie's but I didn't mind, I was in Australia. The only thing I had to do now was to meet all of the family. On the day I got to their home I was really tired out and I guess I was just a little too tired to meet everyone so my auntie phoned them and asked if it could be left till the next morning; I agreed as well. I had something to eat and had a shower and went to bed and slept for sixteen hours so my uncle came in and asked if I was okay. "Still a bit jet lagged," I replied with a very strainful yes.

All my Uncle Phil and Auntie Linda's side of the family were really nice. We got on really well and I wished I could have stayed with them for the rest of my life. I spent most of my time with this family during the time I was in Australia. But there was also my Uncle Derrick and Auntie Eileen, whom I also really liked. My Uncle Derrick was a bit of a grumpy old soul, but I guess you have to take the rough with the smooth. When I was at his seventieth birthday party, my other cousin was supposed to pick me up but Uncle Derrick came and collected me. It takes my Uncle Fred about five minutes to get from his house to Derrick's, but when Derrick came to Uncle Phil's house, it took us twenty minutes to get back to his house. Even though he had been living there for some time, I got the feeling he didn't really know the place too well, bless him. He was a legend behind the wheel. When we pulled off from where I had been staying, Auntie Linda was there watching as we left. With my leg still hanging out the passenger door, I noticed my auntie was looking a bit worried, and as if to say help she just stood there in amazement. It was his birthday after all. Anyway when we finally got going, I said, "How are you, Uncle Derrick?" Then came this stern voice, "Don't call me Uncle Derrick, just call me Derrick." Yes, sir, I thought. I thought he would have liked me to call him my uncle, but then again, maybe it just made him feel older than he was. From then on I didn't really feel comfortable in his company. When I met the other side of my family on "Derricks" birthday, I was again a bit in awe. I was there to meet the rest of my cousins, but as I didn't eat all that much, I think it offended Derrick a little. From then on you could cut the atmosphere with a knife. I felt like walking out of there as Derrick made me feel really small for not eating at his party. Maybe I was the one in the wrong—but never mind, because after all I didn't fly twelve thousand miles for more grief. I can get that back home.

When I was over there, I went to Sidney for three days to meet some of my cousin's friends. They are an Italian family, Maria and Bruce. One conversation I was waiting for was the fact that I was a POME (Prisoner of Mother England). When I first heard this, I thought it was quite funny but as I spent more time over there, it was hard for me to accept that I had to go back to a miserable country where there is nothing but violence. I once heard Tony Blair on television stating that in England we are all free; well, I happen to disagree with that. No, whatever the government decides is best for this country, no matter what the people of England think, we have to like it or lump it.

Knowing what they had in Australia with such a good life and where I never saw any violence and everyone was very friendly—all this made it worse. I liked spending time with my family; it gave me the chance to get to know them better. I did want to be on my own for a while and explore for myself so I booked three days in Melbourne. This was another thing I felt was something I needed to do and was really proud of myself for doing it. I spent one day by the riverside sitting on a bench reflecting on all the things I have accomplished in my life, which wasn't a great deal. For about an hour, I thought of where I went wrong but it's like diving into a pool of oil, dark and lonely, so I thought it best not to go there again. I know one thing—I left a part of myself on that riverside that day and I'll never forget it.

On one of the nights I was there, it was my Auntie and Uncle's fiftieth wedding anniversary. As I was sitting there, I couldn't help feeling jealous of them all and when I had that feeling, I felt that I didn't belong there with them and I felt like a right asshole. I was uncomfortable for the rest of the night. How could I think so low—they had worked really hard for what they got. Why did I feel this way when I was in the company of the perfect family and I just wanted it for my family too. My family got dealt the worse hand in the pack, but I guess that's just life. When I felt really uncomfortable, they must have sensed that things weren't quite right with how I was feeling on that night.

On my last night everyone came round to say goodbye, which was really comforting. The morning after, my uncle and auntie drove me back to the Sidney airport. I bought some souvenirs for the family back home. When it was time to leave, I gave my uncle and auntie a big hug and my auntie had a few tears in her eyes, which almost made me have some. The one thing I was looking forward to the most was when my uncle and auntie would get flowers I ordered them when they weren't looking. When we finally got in the air, I looked back and had a strange feeling, but I couldn't think why and I still don't today. When we dropped down in Japan, I didn't have a hotel to stay in and I ended up sleeping in the airport for sixteen hours, which to be honest I really enjoyed. I phoned home on the night I got there. I told my mum that I didn't have a hotel room and it worried her to death and now that I look back on it I shouldn't have told her. There was this guy in the airport who gave me some assistance on how get in touch with my mum back home. Thanks, dude.

When I saw England I had this really warm feeling of being home and was glad to be back. Why did I feel this way, since I hate England. I think it was the fact that I was going to see my mum and dad again. When I saw their faces in the bus station, I was really excited to tell them about everything and everywhere I'd seen and been. They both had tears in their eyes when they saw me, which also made me happy to be back.

A Brighter Day

When I look back at all the struggles I've come face to face with, I realize that I've had a hard life. I didn't eat gold and have a flying pony, not like some people. I'd sooner forget everything that I've been through. I don't want to remember; it just makes it too painful when I do. Now I want to give myself a better life, than the one I've already been having.

Its time for a change.

I should be dead right now but I'm not for some reason. Most people would have given up by now—not me, though. I seem to have this invisible driving force that keeps me going. When I've felt like giving in, it's like there is someone who grabs me by my wrist and says, "You're not giving up, even if I have to drag you there myself." Is it fate? Some people say everything happens for a reason. I've had severe bouts of depression, suffered from anxiety attacks, and I've been to the hospital for suspected heart attacks—and everything happens for a reason? Personally I'm not sure if that is entirely true. When I sought counseling from a professional, I thought I was at a turning point in my life but as I was thinking that, it was like this voice had said, "No, you're not." It completely sabotaged everything I had hoped for and the only way I was heading was back to the bottom of the barrel.

One rainy day I just wanted to go for a walk. When I was about to leave, my dad asked if I wanted some company but I said that I was heading for Cadbury Hill. "Maybe not," he replied. As I left, I could feel my mum and dad watching me as I left the house, concerned for me but frustrated that there was nothing they could do for me. Imagine how I felt. I know I had to change or else I might have done something bad to myself. I went to my doctor's to get some breathing space as I was receiving sponsorship from the government at the time. They kept pushing and pushing for me to find work but I found this all too stressful. There was a lady that I had an appointment with. She said to me that maybe I needed some time out to get my head together. When she said that, I was almost in tears and it was a job to fight them back, but I managed to.

I watch television and listen to the radio and I see and hear all these musicians sing about how bad their lives are when actually they have good lives. They sing their songs as if they have been in them and nine times out of ten they haven't but they want to. I sit there and think to myself that they must be out of their tiny little minds. After everything that I have been through and they want that for themselves? Well, let the fires of hell drop down on them and let them have a taste of what has happened to me! Then maybe they will think twice about looking a gift horse in the mouth.

There are still so many aspects of my life that I have missed talking about in this book, but I think it's best left where they are.

Things seem to be getting better at the moment. It's going to be a slow and arduous climb but I wouldn't have gotten here without all my friends and my family. I'm not going to give up. I've got this book to complete and I really want to publish this to see where this all takes me. There is hope.

After all I have been through, I've made it to the other end.

Then again, with the experiences I've been through, anything can happen.

Do You Remember the Time

Do you remember the time
You were stood on the porch
The sky was all pink
As we stood there and talked
The clouds were all scattered
As they floated in the air
As we looked up
Could be some rain there
Red sky at night
Shepherds delight
But it rained in the morning
So it was the shepherd's warning.

Do you remember the time
When I was stung by the wasps
I was in so much pain and agony
I walked through the field but I couldn't breathe.
Suddenly I fainted and fell to my knees.
When I awoke, you were the first one there
You put your hand on my head,
As you stood there and stared
You gave me a cuddle
And showed me you cared.
The love will never die
The love that we shared.

Do you remember the time
When we went to Newport
In the pouring rain?
I would continuously do that
Again and again.
I'll never forget it
When we were together
That memory will stay with me
Forever and ever,
I drank the coffee
And you, lime and bicardi.
That was a great day
And forever it will stay.

Have a Drink on Me

It makes me violent
It makes me scream
It even gives me
Nasty dreams
I want to forget it
I wanna let go
It makes my head blurry
Even my reflexes
Are dangerously slow
I'm not myself
I'm not on the ball
And the worst thing of all
I'm vulnerable.

It is my enemy
It is my friend
What a relationship
To the bitter end
As I look around
I can see it's a trend
But it ruins your life.
How can it be
That I like it so much
Oh, now I see
It's an addiction.
No, seriously.

I'm under your spell
What a great feeling
When I wake in the morning
I wake up to hell
Makes me feel low
Makes me feel dark
Makes me feel depressed
Take a long look at yourself
Just like clockwork
In this mindset
I never feel my best
I feel like a monster

No longer can I feel like this
I gotta get stronger

It feels like sleeping with the enemy.
How much I despise you
I sit here and I drink you.
O god how I hate you,
Had some good times
Had some good memories
What wasn't great
Was the headaches
And the hands shake
The arguments and the feuds.
My mind's been abused
A twenty-year struggle
But not anymore
It turned into depression
To the very core
Now I've got rid of you.
Will I go back to you—
No I don't think so
Not anymore
Now I'm taken over
By someone much stronger
Goodbye to you.

It Makes Me Sick

Sick of All This

Turn your back on them
You just know that they hiss
When you put them in their place.
They will not reply to you
No, not to your face.
They would rather do it behind your back,
Stab you in the back.
They are not worth the time of day
People prove me wrong
Every single day
All a' you.
If it's going to be this way
Then there's not much point in me bothering with you.

Sick of all That

When I look back
I know how I felt
I was sick of all that
It was like standing in the middle
of a destruction-derby track.
Back then it did feel like getting run over by a big truck,
I did witness my mum getting drunk
I did witness my mum puking up blood
I did witness my mum taking too many prescription drugs
I bet you're really pleased with yourself coming up trumps
Giving me a three-course meal of nothing but bad luck.
Aren't you tired—haven't you had enough,
I don't like swearing very much
But in this case go and get fucked.

Sick of It All

Sick of talking about it all
Somehow I feel like it's always my fault
I talk about this, I talk about that
I can talk about it until I'm blue in the face.
But yet I still don't know what I'm talking about
You're wrong, I'm right
Nothing in colour
Just black and white
End of conversation
End of this chat
At the end of it all
Forget about all that.
And that the best thing I can do
Is not even talk to you.
Me, Myself, and Lee

Me, Myself, and Lee

Me

Life moves at an incredible rate
So hard to anticipate
Constantly in my face
Makes me question
My whole existence,
Watch this out of control rat race.
I want to create
The perfect life for myself
So far out of reach
So far out of my grasp
This is something I've learned to look past.
Ain't life just one big kick in the ass.
In the end
All you can do is laugh.

Myself

I'm still growing
I am still learning
Deep down inside
There is something
That I am still yearning
A desire for leaving
This thought that I'm having
I feel like wandering
Put some clothes into a bag
Grab a survival knife
And go off traveling
Into the wilderness
Hear the sounds of the trees
As they sway in the breeze
All the birds whistling,
What a calming sound.
I could live here for eternity.

Lee

Back to reality
I hear this little voice
It says
Just get on with it, Lee
Pull your invisible skin over
Out comes this person
With multiple personalities.
Are you ready—
Here we go
1, 2, 3
Funny me
Seriously
So sarcastically.
Who do I really wanna be,
I want to remain all three
Having the same thoughts.
Here we go again, Lee.
Having all these feelings
What a catch 22.
Until the next time
But hey
What can you do.

My Shell

When I was born
I was open and free
I remember the time
When I was happy
But as I grew up
Life wasn't what it seemed
Put my quilt over my head
As I heard all the screams.

Everybody fights
Everybody screams
A normal way of life
Even in my dreams
This way of life
Can push you to the extreme
And this is an experience
That happened to me.

I moved away from home
And became a recluse
As a result of my own
Mental abuse.
You start to tell yourself things
And believe them to be true
Such a horrible way of thinking
From an innocent young youth.
As I get older
So does my shell
No one can penetrate me
Not even in hell.

I hope I'll be happy
I hope I'll be free
I've had enough of this life
Humiliating me
I don't want these walls
That completely surround me
I want to be a free spirit
For all eternity.

No, Really

This is my word
It's a word I've incurred
It's a word I've secured
Some people think it's absurd.
Stop saying that, Lee—
Don't be a jerk
Are you being funny
Are you being sarcastic
However you wanna take it
Don't be offended by it.
But if you don't like it
There's not much I can do about it.

Some people copy me
But in my mind
It will always be mine
A word that shines
Imprinted in my mind
A word that I like
A word that is liked.
To all of my friends
Keep this word going
To the very end.

It's printed in my skin
So very thin
Got to be done again
It's got to stand out
It's got to come out
Every single day
It comes out to play
Every time that I say
The word that I crave
I've said for so long
This word is so strong
It craves me
Me, Myself, and Lee.
This is my word
No, Really.

Stella

You are a great person
I'll love you forever
Our love will never die
Not ever and never.
I remember the day when you came into my life
I will always remember
It's something I'll cherish
Forever and ever.
You've been a huge part of my life
You've been like a mother
Those words were not right—
You have been a mother.

Stella, Stella
Just because I don't say it
Doesn't mean I don't mean it
Because I don't say it
It's because I don't want to lose you
That's why I don't call you mother.
I hope you understand now
But in my mind
There will never be
Another Stella.

I don't know what else to say
But believe me when I say
For every loving day
For every smile you have bought my way
For every hug and kiss on the cheek
Deep down I can see
There is something in me
That wishes
That you gave birth to me
It doesn't matter that you didn't
Because you will always
Be the same to me
My mother for all eternity.

I love you, Stella,
Don't you ever forget that.
You've done so much for me
I'll never forget it.
If ever you need me
You only have to say
We are a family
Forever it will stay.

To Life

From a young child
I grew into a man.
For all that you've thrown at me
I've coped the best that I can.
From the tender age of twelve
I became broken hearted
When cancer took my brother,
We are forever departed.

For all that you gave to me
I'll never forgive you.
A year and twelve days after.
Life, I forbid you,
You took away my mother
What did you think you were doing—
I knew she wouldn't survive
From all the blood she was spewing.

Life, how can you be so relentless
And you keep attacking.
Don't you know I'm defenseless,
Please give me a break
All you seem to do is take,
Take, take, take.
It's fourteen years after
And still you won't quit
You take my last brother
My brother Chris.

I feel tired and broken
I hit rock bottom
I can't see my way
I bring a counselor
Into the fray.
But that didn't work,
I need another helping hand
And she goes by the name of
Dr. Feuchtwang
And a big thank you too,
Citalopram.

I Wish

I wish this world wasn't so real
I wish I didn't have these extraordinary feelings that I feel
I wish my life didn't feel like a card game. Okay dealer deal.
I wish my pain would heal faster
I wish I felt like my life wasn't such a disaster
I wish it didn't happen to me
I wish I didn't have all these feelings of not wanting to be me
I wish these feelings would just leave me
I wish I wasn't in this situation
But you are a fighter, a survivor
You know what you are, you know don't you, Lee.

I wish I didn't feel sadness
I wish I didn't feel anger
I wish I didn't feel pain
I wish I didn't feel bitterness
I wish I didn't have all these feelings
Over and over and over again.
I wish all these feelings would just go away
Go on just go get lost
Go bother someone else and get out of my face.

I wish I watched *Terminator 3*
I wish I took that opportunity
I went to the cinema with you
I'm glad I shared Newport with you
I wish you didn't have to go through all that shit
that you went through.
I know you're at peace now.
I wish that I knew I was going to see you
I wish I didn't walk out that day.
I got a lot of wishes I want to say
If I do that
I'll end up with a three-page essay.
I wish I knew what the future holds for me
I know I have to wait
Any more bad situations I'm gonna anticipate.

I wish I didn't think about all these bad feelings
I wish I didn't write about them
I wish it didn't annoy you
I wish you could understand the situation that I've been through
I wish all these feelings would end soon
I wish I didn't write all these same poem,
They will end soon.
Ok Mum, ok Dad—
Just give me some time.
There will come a time
Then everything will be just fine.

I Didn't Mean It but I Did

I don't ever want to get married
I don't ever want a wife
I don't ever want a kid
I didn't mean it but I did.
Be careful what you wish for,
It just might happen in your future.

There's something about having these feelings
These words that I've just said
I didn't mean them but I did
I definitely did
But I'm not sure it's something I can go through with
For reasons I know that exist.
So I'm sorry for this—
I don't really want to talk about it anymore
I didn't mean it but I did.

For all of you who read this
Please don't take my word for it.
I've just written it
It's just the way that I feel sometimes.
So don't take any notice
Please try to understand.
You now know that I've thought a great deal about this
I didn't mean it but I did.
Where is my ungratefulness—
Did you think I was joking
Did you think I was taking "the" piss.
Oh, I'm sorry I wasn't for real,
I didn't mean it but I did.

Depression, Panic Attack, and Anxiety

This world can be so rough
So tough
This life is no joke
I choke
One bloke
Pain soaked
I'm shy
I cry
I've realized
I'm in love with my sorrow
Good night
I'm going to sleep now
And I'll see you tomorrow.

This life can grind you down
On your face it leaves a constant frown
Inside your chest
My heart beats a painful pound
The more you worry
It leads to more stress
There's nothing you can do about it.
It's like a snowball effect
Your heart feels like a time bomb
Waiting to explode and leave a fat hole outside your chest.
Breathe into a brown paper bag
To try and catch your breath
Inhale, exhale that carbon dioxide
Waiting for it to end.
Here I lay in bed
Waiting for this to end
But it doesn't so I'm going to pretend.

The more I've come to realize
This is not what I want from life
I get this from a constant barrage of problems
I just ignore this
It seeps deeper into my mind.
I'm not looking for a way to solve them
So my thoughts get worse

Leaving me reeling from what I'm feeling.
A normal person would be screaming.
I think I'm cut off from my feelings,
Deep down I know that I'm twisted.
These thoughts leave me angry and frustrated.
This whole whirlwind of bricks—
I never thought to anticipate it
I never saw it coming
It's like a predator
Stealthy and cunning
More deep dark thoughts of wanting to be inconsolable
I know that, that's what's responsible.

This poem is for all the happy people.
Here you go, honey, flower, sweetheart, and treacle
Let's all be happy
Come on, seriously—
You want me to be dizzy and sappy
I have so much resilience
But I'm not giving in,
None of you are coming in.
But now let's see,
Depression
Panic Attacks
And Anxiety—
You won't get me
Even if I'm reincarnated
In the next century.